Quotable Quotes

THE BOOK LOVER

Quotable Quotes

THE BOOK LOVER

Magpie Books

LONDON

Constable & Robinson Ltd
3 The Lanchesters
162 Fulham Palace Road
London W6 9ER
www.constablerobinson.com

This edition published by Magpie Books,
an imprint of Constable & Robinson Ltd 2004

ISBN 1 84529 054 2

Compiled and designed by Tony and Penny Mills

A copy of the British Library Cataloguing in Publications Data
is available from the British Library

Printed and bound in the EU

Contents

Books – A Love Affair

*W*ELCOME TO THE WORLD *of the imagination with a ticket to travel wherever you want. Slay dragons; fall in love; voyage throughout history or just enjoy a good chuckle ...*

What a delicious thing reading is – not to be you any more but to flow through the whole universe you're reading about.

GUSTAVE FLAUBERT
(1821–80)

A good book is the purest essence of the human soul.

THOMAS CARLYLE
(1795–1881)

Here with a loaf of bread beneath a bough,
A flask of wine, a book of verse – and Thou
Beside me singing in the wilderness –
Oh, wilderness were paradise enow.

The Rubáiyát of Omar Khayyám
translated EDWARD FITZGERALD
(1812–70)

There is no Frigate like a Book
To take us Lands away
Nor any Coursers like a Page
Of prancing Poetry.

EMILY DICKINSON
(1830–86)

These are called books. These are the
    strangest things
Thou yet hast seen. I take one of them down,
And lo! a learned dead man comes from his
    grave,
Sits in my chair and holds discourse with me.

JOHN HUNTER-DUVAR
(b. 1830)

Books are not absolutely dead things, but do not contain a potency of life in them to be as active as that soul was whose progeny they are; nay they do preserve as in a vial the purest efficacy and extraction of that living intellect that bred them.

JOHN MILTON
(1608–74)

A good book is the best of friends, the same today and forever.

Proverbial Philosophy Series
MARTIN TUPPER
(1810–89)

I enjoy books as misers delight in wealth, because I know I can enjoy them whensoever I please.

MICHEL DE MONTAIGNE
(1533–92)

In books I find the dead as if they were alive; in books I foresee things to come; in books war-like affairs are set forth; from books come forth the laws of peace. All things are corrupted and decay in time; Saturn ceases not to devour the children that he generates; all the glory of the world would be buried in oblivion, unless God had provided mortals with the remedy of books.

The Love of Books
RICHARD DE BURY
(1281–1345)

It is only through daily reading that you refresh your mind sufficiently to speak wisely.

Books, books, books!
I had found the secret of a garret-room
Piled high with cases in my father's name;
Piled high, packed large, – where, creeping in and out
Among the giant fossils of my past,
Like some small nimble mouse between the ribs
Of a mastodon, I nibbled here and there
At this or that box, pulling through the gap,
In heats of terror, haste, victorious joy,
The first book first. And how I felt it beat
Under my pillow, in the morning's dark,
An hour before the sun would let me read!

From 'Aurora Leigh'
ELIZABETH BARRETT BROWNING
(1806–61)

A book is a friend whose face is constantly changing. If you read it when you are recovering from an illness, and return to it years after, it is changed surely, with the change in yourself.

The Library
ANDREW LANG
(1844–1912)

Good friends, good books and a sleepy conscience: this is the ideal life.

MARK TWAIN
(1835–1910)

'Although she has been advised to take exercise, she prefers always sitting in her room reading.'

'Like me,' replied Leon. 'And indeed, what is better than to sit by one's fireside in the evening with a book, while the wind beats against the window and the lamp is burning?'

'What, indeed?' she said, fixing her large black eyes wide open upon him.

'One thinks of nothing,' he continued; 'the

hours slip by. Motionless we traverse countries we fancy we see, and your thought, blending with the fiction, playing with the details, follows the outline of the adventures. It mingles with the characters, and it seems as if it were yourself palpitating beneath their costumes.'

Madame Bovary
GUSTAVE FLAUBERT
(1821–80)

If only I could manage, without annoyance to my family, to get imprisoned for 10 years, 'without hard labour,' and with the use of books and writing materials, it would be simply delightful!

LEWIS CARROLL
(1832–98)

B ooks, the children
of the brain.

JONATHAN SWIFT
(1667–1745)

B ooks, gentlemen, are a species of men, and
introduced to them you circulate in the 'very
best society' that this world can furnish, without
the intolerable infliction of 'dressing' to go into
it. In your shabbiest coat and cosiest slippers you
may socially chat even with the fastidious Earl of
Chesterfield, and lounging under a tree enjoy the
divinest intimacy with my late lord of Verulam.

HERMAN MELVILLE
(1819–91)

B ooks are the bees which carry the quickening
pollen from one to another mind.

JAMES RUSSELL LOWELL
(1819–91)

Old books to read!
Ay, bring those nodes of wit,
The brazen-clasped, the vellum writ,
　　Time-honored tomes!
The same my sire scanned before,
The same my grandsire thumbèd o'er,
The same his sire from college bore,
　The well-earned meed
　　Of Oxford's domes:
　　Old Homer blind,
Old Horace, rake Anacreon, by
Old Tully, Plautus, Terence lie;
Mort Arthur's olden minstrelsie,
Quaint Burton, quainter Spenser, ay!
And Gervase Markham's venerie –
　　Nor leave behind
The holye Book by which we live and die.

　　　　From 'A Winter Wish'
　　　　Robert Hinckley Messinger
　　　　　(1811–74)

Books are quiet. They do not dissolve into wavy lines or snowstorm effects. They do not pause to deliver commercials. They are three-dimensional, having length, breadth and depth. They are convenient to handle and completely portable.

ANON.

Chaucer is fresh and modern still, and no dust settles on his true passages. It lightens along the line, and we are reminded that flowers have bloomed, and birds sung, and hearts beaten in England. Before the earnest gaze of the reader, the rust and moss of time gradually drop off, and the original green life is revealed. He was a homely and domestic man, and did breathe quite as modern men do.

A Week on the Concord and Merrimack Rivers
HENRY DAVID THOREAU
(1817–62)

I had rather be shut up in a very modest cottage, with my books, my family and a few old friends, dining on simple bacon, and letting the world roll on as it liked, than to occupy the most splendid post which any human power can give.

THOMAS JEFFERSON
(1743–1826)

There are only three pleasures in life pure and lasting, and all derived from inanimate things – books, pictures and the face of nature.

Criticisms on Art
WILLIAM HAZLITT
(1778–1830)

Readers Encouraged and Admonished

*I*T MAY NOT BE POSSIBLE to meet our *favourite writers, but on a summer's day we can sit in a deckchair and listen to their words in our hearts, or in the winter cuddle up in front the fire with an old friend ...*

A reader seldom peruses a book with pleasure until he knows whether the writer of it be a black man or a fair man, of a mild or choleric disposition, married or a bachelor.

The Spectator
JOSEPH ADDISON
(1672–1719)

Some books are to be tasted, others to be swallowed, and some few to be chewed and digested …

Essays
FRANCIS
(1561–1626)

I have met with women whom I really think would like to be married to a poem and to be given away by a novel.

JOHN KEATS
(1795–1821)

Lectures, sir! what man would go to hear that imperfectly at a lecture, which he can read at leisure in a book?

SAMUEL JOHNSON
(1709–84)

It is better to be able neither to read nor write than to be able to do nothing else. A lounger who is ordinarily seen with a book in his hand is (we may be almost sure) equally without the power or inclination to attend either to what passes around him or in his own mind. Such a

one may be said to carry his understanding about with him in his pocket, or to leave it at home on his library shelves.

Table-Talk Essays on Men and Manners
WILLIAM HAZLITT
(1778–1830)

All books are either dreams or swords, you can cut, or you can drug, with words.

'Sword Blades and Poppy Seed'
AMY LOWELL
(1874–1925)

Reading and marriage do not always make happy bedfellows .

Les Femmes Savante
JOHN-BAPTISTE POQUELIN MOLIÈRE
(1622–73)

The greatest delight in the world is to have met a woman who will allow me to read in peace until it's time for bed.

The White Man's Burden
JOSIAH MILLER
(1880–1934)

It is easy to buy a book; what is more difficult is to purchase the time in which to read them. Too often the mere fact of possession tempts us to think we own the contents.

ARTHUR SCHOPENHAUER
(1788–1860)

As for the furniture of the rooms ... on the table a multiplicity of those little gilt books, half sentimental and half religious, which the wants of the age and of our young ladies have produced in such numbers of late. I quarrel with no lady's taste in that way; but heigho! I had rather that Mrs. Fitz-Boodle should read *Humphry Clinker*!

Besides these works, there was a *Peerage*, of course. What genteel family was ever without one?

Men's Wives
WILLIAM MAKEPEACE THACKERAY
(1811–63)

Be sure that you go to the author to get at his meaning, not to find yours.

JOHN RUSKIN
(1819–1900)

Take thou a book into thine hands as Simon the Just took the child Jesus into his arms to carry him and kiss him and when thou hast finished reading, close the book and give thanks for every word out of the mouth of God; because in the Lord's field thou hast found a hidden treasure.

Doctrinale Juvenum
THOMAS À KEMPIS
(1380–1471)

What a sense of security in an old book which Time has criticised for us!

JAMES RUSSELL LOWELL.
(1819–91)

When you read a book there are only three things of which you may be conscious:

(1) The significance of the words, which is inseparably bound up with the thought.

(2) The look of the printed words on the page – I do not suppose that anybody reads any author for the visual beauty of the words on the page.

(3) The sound of the words, either actually uttered or imagined by the brain to be uttered. Now it is indubitable that words differ in beauty of sound.

Literary Taste – How to Form It
ARNOLD BENNETT
(1867–1931)

Her reading fared like her piece of embroidery, all of which, only just begun, filled her cupboard; she took it up, left it, passed on to other books.

Madame Bovary
GUSTAVE FLAUBERT
(1821–80)

Books are fatal: they are the curse of the human race. Nine-tenths of existing books are nonsense, and the clever books are the refutation of that nonsense. The greatest misfortune that ever befell man was the invention of printing.

Lothair
BENJAMIN DISRAELI
LORD BEACONSFIELD
(1804–81)

All books are divisible into two classes: the books of the hour, and the books of all time.

JOHN RUSKIN
(1819–1900)

Most good books have begun by causing anger which disguised itself as contempt. Demanding honesty from your authors, you must see that you render it yourself. And to be honest with oneself is not so simple as it appears. One's sensations and one's sentiments must be examined with detachment. When you have violently flung down a book, listen whether you can hear a faint voice saying within you: 'It's true, though!' And if you catch the whisper, better yield to it as quickly as you can. For sooner or later the voice will win. Similarly, when you are hugging a book, keep your ear cocked for the secret warning: 'Yes, but it isn't true.' For bad books, by flattering you, by caressing, by appealing to the weak or the base in you, will often persuade you what fine and splendid books they are.

Literary Taste – How to Form It
ARNOLD BENNETT
(1867–1931)

Publish and be damned.

ARTHUR WELLESLEY
DUKE OF WELLINGTON
(1769–1852)

Men formerly plunged into all the vicissitudes and dangers of war, or staked their all upon a single die, or some one passion, which if they could not have gratified, life became a burden to them – now our strongest passion is to think, our chief amusement is to read new plays, new poems, new novels, and this we may do at our leisure, in perfect security, ad infinitum.

Table-Talk Essays on Men and Manners
WILLIAM HAZLITT
(1778–1830)

Society – begging her pardon! – is often a great fool. Why should it be less creditable to make good dresses than bad books?

A Woman's Thoughts About Women
DINAH MARIA MULOCK CRAIK
(1826–87)

A dip into the volume at random and so on for a page or two: and now and then a smile; and presently a gape; and the book drops out of your hand; and so, bon soir, and pleasant dreams to you. I have frequently seen men at clubs asleep over their humble servant's works, and am always pleased. Even at a lecture I don't mind, if they don't snore.

Roundabout Papers
WILLIAM MAKEPEACE THACKERAY
(1811–63)

Discourse was deemed Man's noblest attribute,
And written words the glory of his hand;
Then followed Printing with enlarged command
For thought – dominion vast and absolute
For spreading truth, and making love expand.
Now prose and verse sunk into disrepute
Must lacquey a dumb Art that best can suit
The taste of this once-intellectual Land.
A backward movement surely have we here,
From manhood, – back to childhood; for the age
Back towards caverned life's first rude career.
Avaunt this vile abuse of pictured page!
Must eyes be all in all, the tongue and ear
Nothing? Heaven keep us from a lower stage!

'Illustrated Books and Newspapers'
WILLIAM WORDSWORTH
(1770–1850)

… However, many books,
Wise men have said, are wearisome; who reads
Incessantly, and to his reading brings not
A spirit and judgment equal or superior,
(And what he brings what needs he elsewhere seek?)
Uncertain and unsettled still remains,
Deep-versed in books and shallow in himself,
Crude or intoxicate, collecting toys
And trifles for choice matters, worth a sponge,
As children gathering pebbles on the shore.

Paradise Regained
JOHN MILTON
(1608–74)

Books, like proverbs, receive their chief value
from the stamp and esteem of ages through
which they have passed.

SIR WILLIAM TEMPLE
(1628–99)

Y ou've paid enough for the book; why not save the cost of your postage (and all the time you've spent writing your carping, poorly punctuated, and, as it happens, factually incorrect letter) and think to yourself, 'What good am I doing to the world by ruining this poor writer's morning?'

20TH–CENTURY AUTHOR

B ooks cannot always please, however good; Minds are not ever craving for their food.

GEORGE CRABBE
(1754–1832)

B ooks describe customs and morals; books do
not prescribe them.

THEOPHILE GAUTIER
(1811–72)

B ooks are for the most part willfully and
hastily written, as parts of a system to
supply a want real or imagined.

HENRY DAVID THOREAU
(1817–62)

N o entertainment is so cheap as reading, nor
any pleasure so lasting. She will not want
new fashions nor regret the loss of expensive
diversions or variety of company if she can be
amused with an author in her closet.

LADY MARY WORTLEY MONTAGU
(1689–1762)

In books one finds golden palaces and maidens as beautiful as jewels.

CHINESE PROVERB

If you wish to understand the past read a poem or a novel or a contemporary life. Historians pervert the clarity of a reader's vision.

TRUISM

2004

Books are the best things, well used; abused, among the worst. What is the right use? What is the one end, which all means go to effect? They are for nothing but to inspire. I had better never see a book, than to be warped by its attraction clean out of my own orbit, and made a satellite instead of a system.

RALPH WALDO EMERSON

(1803–1882)

33

Writers whose thoughts are expressed with clarity and precision are assumed by readers to be superficial. Where the meaning is obscured; then readers give more attention and consider the fruit of their labour more valuable

FRIEDRICH NIETZSCHE
(1844–1900)

Reading is purloining another person's thoughts, instead of thinking with one's own head.

ARTHUR SCHOPENHAUER
(1788–1860)

Solitude, reading, laziness, a gentle and leisured life, socialising too much with women and young people, these are dangerous habits for a young person, and lead him or her constantly into temptation.

Émile
JEAN-JACQUES ROUSSEAU
(1712–78)

Never read any book that is not a year old.

RALPH WALDO EMERSON
(1803–82)

Burton's *Anatomy of Melancholy,* he said, was the only book that ever took him out of bed two hours sooner than he wished to rise.

The Life of Samuel Johnson
JAMES BOSWELL
(1740–95)

A good book is the precious life-blood of a master spirit, embalmed and treasured up on purpose to a life beyond life.

JOHN MILTON
(1608–74)

I envy them, those monks of old; Their books they read, and their beads they told.

G.P.R. JAMES
(1801–60)

In books lies the soul of the whole Past Time: the articulate audible voice of the Past, when the body and material substance of it has altogether vanished like a dream.

THOMAS CARLYLE
(1795–1881)

There is no such thing as a moral or an immoral book. Books are well written, or badly written.

OSCAR WILDE
(1854–1900)

What use is a book that does not even enable us to travel into a land beyond books?

FRIEDRICH NIETZSCHE
(1844–1900)

Children and Books

*W*HEN WE WERE CHILDREN *books carried us into a magic world where everything was possible. While the rain drizzled down outside, or adults mercilessly bored on, we could escape to a sunnier land of dreams and excitement.*

'What is the use of a book' thought Alice,
without pictures or conversations?'

Alice's Adventures in Wonderland
LEWIS CARROLL
(1832–98)

Summer fading, winter comes —
Frosty mornings, tingling thumbs
Window robins, winter rooks,
And the picture story-books.

All the pretty things put by,
Wait upon the children's eye,
Sheep and shepherds, trees and crooks,
In the picture story-books.

How am I to sing your praise,
Happy chimney-corner days,
Sitting safe in nursery nooks,
Reading picture story-books?

from 'Picture-books in Winter'
A Child's Garden of Verses and Underwoods
ROBERT LOUIS STEVENSON
(1850–94)

To the many boys and girls whose letters it has been impossible to answer, this book is dedicated as a peace offering by their friend, L.M.A.

Eight Cousins; or The Aunt-Hill
dedication
LOUISA MAY ALCOTT
(1832–88)

❖

For the long nights you lay awake
And watched for my unworthy sake:
For your most comfortable hand
That led me through the uneven land:
For all the story-books you read:
For all the pains you comforted:
For all you pitied, all you bore,
In sad and happy days of yore: –
My second Mother, my first Wife,
The angel of my infant life –
From the sick child, now well and old,
Take, nurse, the little book you hold!

And grant it, Heaven, that all who read
May find as dear a nurse at need,
And every child who lists my rhyme,
In the bright, fireside, nursery clime,
May hear it in as kind a voice
As made my childish days rejoice!

'To Alison Cunningham
From Her Boy'
A Child's Garden of Verses and Underwoods
ROBERT LOUIS STEVENSON
(1850–94)

Guide to the Use and Purpose of Books in the School Library

1 The primary purpose of a book is not that it should be used as a weapon.

Further: it is no excuse to say:

'We were so inspired by Froissart that we decided to re-enact the Battle of Hastings, but we had no arrows', or similarly,

'Hercules had a giant wooden club; this is just a slim octavo of poetry.'

To say 'It was only a paperback and wouldn't hurt a flea' is also an unacceptable excuse.

2 Every copy of Kennedy's *Shorter Latin Primer* in the school has now been changed to read Kennedy's *'Shortbread Eating Primer'*; you should not waste your whole reading period thinking of imaginative ways to re-title Gibbon's *Decline*

and Fall of the Roman Empire, or whatever other book you are *pretending* to read.

3 You should not write:
'If my name you wish to see
Turn to page one-o-three'
and then write on p.103;
'If my name you wish to know
To page eight, you must go'
and similarly throughout the book until you are bored and tail off with 'Ha, Ha'.

4 Book illustrators are professional artists; you are not. It is not acceptable to say that a moustache adds dignity to Queen Victoria nor a skirt encircling Julius Caesar balances the composition.

5 You should remember that Mrs Curtis-Twigg who replaces me on my day off (Wednesday) is as much a human being as a librarian. You should not obviously cross yourself before entering the library, nor say just outside the door, in intentionally audible voice, 'I've got some onion from the stew at lunch in my pocket; do you think it will work as well as garlic?'

ascribed to Cressbrook School
Kirkby Lonsdale

To my daughter Leonora without whose never-failing sympathy and encouragement, this book would have been finished in half the time.

The Heart of a Goof
dedication
P.G. WODEHOUSE

I never read quite to the end of my first [novel], the *Scottish Chiefs*. I couldn't. I peeped in an alarmed furtive manner at some of the closing pages. Miss Porter, like a kind dear tender-hearted creature, would not have Wallace's head chopped off at the end of Vol. V. She made him die in prison, and if I remember right (protesting I have not read the book for forty-two or three years), Robert Bruce made a speech to his soldiers ... But I repeat I could not read the end of the fifth volume of that dear delightful book for crying. Good heavens! It was as sad, as sad as going back to school.

Roundabout Papers
WILLIAM MAKEPEACE THACKERAY
(1811–63)

After supper she got out her book and learned me about Moses and the Bulrushers; and I was in a sweat to find out all about him; but by and by she let it out that Moses had been dead a considerable long time; so then I didn't care no more about him; because I don't take no stock in dead people.

The Adventures of Huckleberry Finn
MARK TWAIN
(1835–1910)

Don't draw pictures on the page
Of your books, I've told you, Pelham.
One day they'll be all the rage,
And it's then you'll want to sell 'em.

From *Advice to Small Children*
PEREGRINE FINZI
(1870–1973)

Even now that I am over sixty I still shudder when I think of Miss Knox-English. In the depth of February she would stride into the day room and boom 'What sort of girl slouches over a book when there is work to be done? Come and put out the hockey-markers, Penelope'.

Family Memoir
MRS J.A. MONKTON
(1920–99)

They [the books Emma loved] were all love, lovers, sweethearts, persecuted ladies fainting in lonely pavilions, postilions killed at every stage, horses ridden to death on every page, sombre forests, heartaches, vows, sobs, tears and kisses, little skiffs by moonlight, nightingales in shady groves, 'gentlemen' brave as lions, gentle as lambs, virtuous as no one ever was, always well dressed, and weeping like fountains. For six months, then, Emma, at fifteen years of age, made her hands dirty with books from old lending libraries.

Madame Bovary
GUSTAVE FLAUBERT
(1821–80)

C-l-e-a-n, clean, verb active, to make bright, to scour. W-i-n, win, d-e-r, der, winder, a casement. When the boy knows this out of the book, he goes and does it.

Nicholas Nickleby
CHARLES DICKENS
(1812–70)

Is it not strange, that an infant should be heir of the whole world, and see those mysteries which the books of the learned never unfold?

THOMAS TRAHERNE
(1636–74)

It all comes out of the books I read,
And it all goes into the books I write.

HENRY CHARLES BEECHING
(1859–1919)

For what are all our contrivings,
  And the wisdom of our books,
When compared with your caresses,
  And the gladness of your looks?

Ye are better than all the ballads
  That were ever sung or said;
For ye are living poems
  And all the rest are dead!

'The Children's Hour'
HENRY WADSWORTH LONGFELLOW
(1807–82)

I loved reading, and had a great desire of attaining knowledge; but whenever I asked questions of any kind whatsoever, I was always told, 'such things were not proper for girls of my age to know.' … For 'Miss must not enquire too far into things, it would turn her brain; she had better mind her needlework, and such things as were useful for women; reading and poring on books would never get me a husband.'

The Adventures of David Simple
SARAH FIELDING
(1710–68)

Writers on Books

*I*T IS ALWAYS A PLEASURE and an inspiration to listen to a craftsman discussing the work and methods of his fellows with an expert's insight. Here we can eavesdrop as writers discuss the skills of their trade.

The greatest part of a writer's time is spent in reading in order to write: a man will turn over half of a library in order to make one book.

The Life of Samuel Johnson
JAMES BOSWELL
(1740–95)

Books treating of etiquette ... are often written by dancing-masters and Turveydrops and others knowing little of the customs of the best society of any land.

MRS. H. O. WARD
(1824–99)

There is no pleasure like reading a bad review of a fellow author's work, especially if I have written it myself.

A CONTEMPORARY WRITER WHO PREFERS TO REMAIN ANONYMOUS

Books, like men their authors, have no more than one way of coming into the world, but there are ten thousand to go out of it, and return no more.

A Tale of a Tub
JONATHON SWIFT
(1667–1745)

Some books are lies frae end to end.

ROBERT BURNS
(1759–96)

Years ago there was a wretched outcry raised because Mr. Macaulay dated a letter from Windsor Castle, where he was staying. Immortal gods! Was this man not a fit guest for any palace in the world? or a fit companion for any man or woman in it?

Roundabout Papers
WILLIAM MAKEPEACE THACKERAY
(1811–63)

Digressions, incontestably, are the sunshine; – they are the life, the soul of reading; – take them out of the book for instance, – you might as well take the book along with them.

Tristram Shandy
LAURENCE STERNE
(1713–68)

The man who is asked by an author what he thinks of his work, is put to the torture, and is not obliged to speak the truth.

SAMUEL JOHNSON
(1709–84)

Rabelais, for instance, is intolerable; one chapter is better than a volume, – it may be sport to him, but it is death to us. A mere humorist, indeed, is a most unhappy man; and his readers are most unhappy also.

The Writings of Henry David Thoreau
HENRY DAVID THOREAU
(1817–62)

I never knew the *Arabian Nights* was an improper book until I happened once to read it in a 'family edition'.

Roundabout Papers
WILLIAM MAKEPEACE THACKERAY
(1811–63)

The venerable devotion of the religious orders is wont to be solicitous in the care of books and to delight in their society, as if they were the only riches.

For some used to write them with their own hands between the hours of prayer, and gave to the making of books such intervals as they could secure and the times appointed for the recreation of the body.

By whose labours there are resplendent to-day in most monasteries these sacred treasuries full of cherubic letters, for giving the knowledge of salvation to the student and a delectable light to the paths of the laity.

The Love of Books
RICHARD DE BURY
(1281–1345)

A celebrated lyrical writer happened to drop into a small party where they had just got the novel of *Rob Roy* by the author of *Waverley*. The motto in the title-page was taken from a poem of his. This was a hint sufficient, a word to the wise. He instantly went to the book-shelf in the next room, took down the volume of his own poems, read the whole of that in question aloud with manifest complacency, replaced it on the shelf, and walked away, taking no more notice of *Rob Roy* than if there had been no such person, nor of the new novel than if it had not been written by its renowned author. There was no reciprocity in this. But the writer in question does not admit of any merit second to his own.

Table-Talk Essays on Men and Manners
WILLIAM HAZLITT
(1778–1830)

The oldest books are still only just out to those who have not read them.

SAMUEL BUTLER
(1835–1902)

The days of blue-stockings are over: it is a notable fact, that the best housekeepers, the neatest needlewomen, the most discreet managers of their own and others' affairs, are ladies whose names the world cons over in library lists and exhibition catalogues. I could give them now – except that the world has no possible business with them, except to read their books and look at their pictures

A Woman's Thoughts About Women
DINAH MARIA MULOCK CRAIK
(1826–87)

I hate books; they give us a second hand view of the world.

JEAN-JACQUES ROUSSEAU
(1712–78)

Shakespeare is one of the last books one should like to give up, perhaps the one just before the Dying Service in a large Prayer book.

Letter to William Wordsworth
CHARLES LAMB
(1775–1834)

What is written without effort is in general read without pleasure.

SAMUEL JOHNSON
(1709–84)

You write with ease, to show your breeding,
But easy writing's vile hard reading.

'Clio's Protest'
RICHARD BRINSLEY SHERIDAN
(1751–1816)

Books that you may carry to the fire and hold readily in your hand, are the most useful after all.

SAMUEL JOHNSON
(1709–84)

Books that have become classics – books that have had their day and now get more praise than perusal – always remind me of retired colonels and majors and captains who, having reached the age limit, find themselves retired on half pay.

Ponkapog Papers
THOMAS BAILEY ALDRICH
(1836–1907)

Beware of a man of one book.

ROBERT SOUTHEY
(1774–1843)

Newspapers are to blame for so much; they draw our attention to matters which are of no importance beyond the end of the week, but in a book, perhaps only three or four time in a lifetime, we come across ideas that are all-transforming. How wonderful, if when we opened our daily paper, we should find – as it were – the *Pensées* by Pascal!

Remembrance of Things Past
MARCEL PROUST
(1871–1922)

Give me books, fruit, French wine and fine weather and a little music out of doors, played by someone I do not know ... I admire lolling on a lawn by a water-lilied pond to eat white currants and see goldfish: and go to the fair in the evening if I'm good. There is not hope for that – one is sure to get into some mess before evening.

Letter to his sister Fanny
JOHN KEATS
(1795–1821)

It would be worth the while to select our reading, for books are the society we keep; to read only the serenely true; never statistics, nor fiction, nor news, nor reports, nor periodicals, but only great poems, and when they failed, read them again, or perchance write more. Instead of other sacrifice, we might offer up our perfect (teleia) thoughts to the gods daily, in hymns or psalms. For we should be at the helm at least once a day.

HENRY DAVID THOREAU
(1817–62)

This book comes to you openly and honestly, reader. It tells you from the start that, in it, I have no purpose but a private and individual one … I myself am the only subject of my book.

MICHEL DE MONTAIGNE
(1533–92)

Here lies Jonson with the rest
Of the poets; but the best.
Reader, would'st thou more have known?
Ask his story, not this stone.
That will speak what this can't tell
Of his glory. So farewell.

ROBERT HERRICK
(1591–1674)

Book Abuse

NORMALLY PLEASANT AND well-mannered friends seem to lose all sense of morality when dealing with books. They will happily browse through your own collection and then walk off with anthing they fancy. They will handle the most beautiful with greasy fingers. So, before you go round to their houses to wreak revenge, read this and try to calm down.

Worst fate of books, [to] fall into the hands of women who will sell them to the trunk-maker. Are the leaves to line a box or to curl a maiden's locks?

The Library
ANDREW LANG
(1844–1912)

Your borrowers of books – those mutilators of collections, spoilers of the symmetry of shelves, and creators of odd volumes.

Essays of Elia
CHARLES LAMB
(1740–95)

It may be questioned whether, at the burning of the library at Alexandria, there were a hundred volumes utterly lost to the world, which were not more serviceable as fuel for the baths than as food for the mind.

The Book of the Boudoir
LADY MORGAN
1829

One is often tempted to believe, in the great influx of small talents which now deluges us, that if half the books written, and pictures painted, were made into one great bonfire, it would be their shortest, easiest, and safest way of illuminating the world.

A Woman's Thoughts About Women
DINAH MARIA MULOCK CRAIK
(1826–87)

A big leather-bound volume makes an ideal razorstrap. A thin book is useful to stick under a table with a broken caster to steady it. A large, flat atlas can be used to cover a window with a broken pane. And a thick, old-fashioned heavy book with a clasp is the finest thing in the world to throw at a noisy cat.

MARK TWAIN
(1835–1910)

❖

Pest of the Muses, devourer of pages, in crannies
that lurkest,
Fruits of the Muses to taint, labour of learning to
spoil;
Wherefore, oh black-fleshed worm! wert thou
born for the evil thou workest?
Wherefore thine own foul form shap'st thou
with envious toil?

an epigram against the black book-worm
EVENUS, THE GRAMMARIAN

No iron-stained hand is fit to handle books,
Nor he whose heart on gold so gladly looks:
The same men love not books and money both,
And books thy herd, O Epicurus, loathe;
Misers and bookmen make poor company,
Nor dwell in peace beneath the same roof-tree.
No man, therefore, can serve both books and
Mammon.

The Love of Books
RICHARD DE BURY
(1281–1345)

It is a wonder how fond ladies are of writing in books, and signing their charming initials! Mrs. Berry's ... little gilt books are scored with pencil-marks, or occasionally at the margin with a note of interjection, or the words 'TOO TRUE, A.B.' and so on. Much may be learned with regard to lovely woman by a look at the books she reads in; and I had gained no inconsiderable knowledge of Mrs. Berry by the ten minutes spent in the drawing-room, while she was at her toilet in the adjoining bedchamber.

Men's Wives
WILLIAM MAKEPEACE THACKERAY
(1811–63)

Few book-ghouls are worse than the moral ghoul. He defaces, with a pen, the passages, in some precious volume, which do not meet his idea of moral propriety … The antiquarian ghoul steals title-pages and colophons. The aesthetic ghoul cuts illuminated initials out of manuscripts. The petty, trivial, and almost idiotic ghoul of our own days, sponges the fly-leaves and boards of books for the purpose of cribbing the book-plates.

The Library
ANDREW LANG
(1844–1912)

The covetous man who is in the extreme state of book-loving, is the biblioklept, or book-stealer.

The Library
ANDREW LANG
(1844–1912)

'Becky Sharp, here's a book for you that my sister – that is, I – Johnson's Dictionary, you know; you mustn't leave us without that.

Good-by.

Drive on, coachman.

God bless you!'

And the kind creature retreated into the garden, overcome with emotion.

But, lo! and just as the coach drove off, Miss Sharp put her pale face out of the window and actually flung the book back into the garden.

Vanity Fair
WILLIAM MAKEPEACE THACKERAY
(1811–63)

Good books are more more dangerous to the state than bad as they are more likely to be read.

HEINZ HAUSSMANN
(1897–1944)

We deem it expedient to warn our students of various negligences, which might be easily avoided and do great harm to books. For it behoves us to guard a book much more carefully than a boot.

The race of scholars is commonly badly brought up, and unless they are bridled in by the rules of their elders they indulge in infinite puerilities ...

A headstrong youth who when the winter's frost is sharp, his nose running from the nipping cold drips down, does not think of wiping it with his pocket-handkerchief until he has bedewed the book before him with the ugly moisture.

His nails are stuffed with fetid filth as black as jet, with which he marks any passage that pleases him.

He does not fear to eat fruit or cheese over an open book, or carelessly to carry a cup to and from his mouth.

Now the rain is over and the flowers have appeared in our land. The scholar will stuff his volume with violets, and primroses, with roses and quatrefoil.

Then he will use his wet and perspiring hands to open the volumes; then it is not shut for another month, until it is so full of dust that it resists the effort to close it.

The handling of books is specially to be forbidden to those who when they find an extra margin, furnish it with monstrous alphabets.

Let the clerk take care also that the smutty scullion reeking from his stewpots does not touch the lily leaves of books.

And, again, the cleanliness of decent hands would be of great benefit to books as well as scholars, if it were not that the itch and pimples are characteristic of the clergy.

The Love of Books
RICHARD DE BURY
(1281–1345)

BOOK BURNIG IN THE GREAT FIRE

Mr Kirton's kinsman, my bookseller, come in my way; and so I am told by him that Mr Kirton is utterly undone, and made 2 or 3000*l.* worse than nothing, from being worth 7 or 8000*l.* That the goods laid in a Church-yard fired through the windows those in St. Fayth's church; and those coming to the warhouses' doors fired them, and burnt all the books and the pillars of the church, so as the roof falling down, broke quite down; which it did not do in the other places of the church. He do believe there is above 150,000*l.* of books burnt; all the great booksellers almost undone: not only these, but their warehouse at their Hall and under Christ-church, and elsewhere, being all burned. A great want thereof there will be of books, specially Latin books and foreign books; and, among others, the polyglottes and new Bible, which he believes will be presently worth 40*l.* a-piece.

Diary, 5th October 1666
SAMUEL PEPYS
(1633–1703)

I knew a gentleman who was so good a manager of his time that he would not even lose that small portion of it which the calls of nature obliged him to pass in the necessary-house; but gradually went through all the Latin poets in those moments. He bought, for example, a common edition of Horace, of which he tore off gradually a couple of pages, carried them with him to that necessary place, read them first, and then sent them down as a sacrifice to Cloacina. [The Roman goddess of the lavatory]

The Letters of the Earl of Chesterfield
to his Son.
LORD CHESTERFIELD
(1694—1773)

When I had hounds and credit, and grave friends
To borrow my books and set wet glasses on them.

EDWIN ARLINGTON ROBINSON
(1869–1935)

A nother enemy of books must be mentioned with the delicacy that befits the topic. Almost all women are the inveterate foes, not of novels, of course, nor peerages and popular volumes of history, but of books worthy of the name. It is true that Isabelle d'Este, and Madame de Pompadour, and Madame de Maintenon, were collectors; and, doubtless, there are other brilliant exceptions to a general rule. But, broadly speaking, women detest the books which the collector desires and admires. First, they don't understand them; second, they are jealous of their mysterious charms; third, books cost money; and it really is a hard thing for a lady to see money expended on what seems a dingy old binding, or yellow paper scored with crabbed characters.

The Library
ANDREW LANG
(1844–1912)

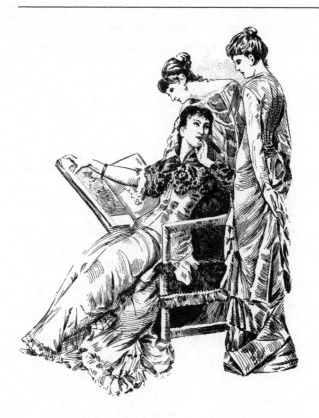

It is as permissible now to make love to the wives of others as it is to smoke their cigarettes or read their books.

ANTON PAVLOVICH CHEKHOV
(1860–1904)

A ravenous student called Frost
For pudding had *Paradise Lost*
He declared he found Milton
As tasty as Stilton
And selling for a half of the cost.

P.J.M.

Books may be burned and cities sacked, but truth like the yearning for freedom, lives in the hearts of humble men and women. The ultimate victory, the ultimate victory of tomorrow is with democracy; and true democracy with education, for no people in all the world can be kept eternally ignorant or eternally enslaved.

FRANKLIN D. ROOSEVELT
(1882–1945)
(recordings of Franklin Roosevelt's
public addresses)

They lard their lean books with the fat of others' works.

ROBERT BURTON
(1577–1640)

Above the lintel of his library door, Pixerecourt had this couplet carved:

> Tel est le triste sort de tout livre prete,
> Souvent il est perdu, toujours il est gate.
> [Such is the tragic outcome of all books taken,
> Often it is lost, always it is spoilt]

Quoted in *The Library*
ANDREW LANG
(1844—1912)

The Collector and The Trade

*O*F COURSE, WE mustn't judge a book by its cover and one of the greatest delights in life is to discover a volume we have often wished to read, forgotten on an undusted shelf in the back room of a second-hand booksellers, for sale at a knock-down price. It is equally pleasing, though, to feel the craftsmanship of an old leather bound tome as it rests in our own hands.

Of making many books there is no end; and much study is a weariness of the flesh.

ECCLESIASTES
Bible

Books, books again, and books once more!
These are our theme, which some miscall
Mere madness, setting little store
By copies either short or tall.
But you, O slaves of shelf and stall!
We rather write for you that hold
Patched folios dear, and prize 'the small,
Rare volume, black with tarnished gold.'

A. D.
1881

A well-bound book ... has its price, even if its literary contents be of trifling value.

The Library
ANDREW LANG
(1844–1912)

There is ... a recent instance of a Rugby boy, who picked up, on a stall, a few fluttering leaves hanging together on a flimsy thread. The old woman who kept the stall could hardly be induced to accept the large sum of a shilling for an original quarto of Shakespeare's *King John*.

The Library
ANDREW LANG
(1844–1912)

A collector I know, name of Green
On art books excessively keen,
Is, at present, inside
'Cause his joy and his pride
Was seized by the fuzz as obscene.

P.J.M.

82

There are men who write and produce books, then send them out into the world, with as much speed as they would produce a fried egg.

MIGUEL DE CERVANTES SAAVEDRA
(1547–1616)

Hack: one whose services are for hire; especially a literary drudge, compiler, furbisher of better men's work. Goldsmith, who knew well from his own experience, what the work was like, wrote:

'Here lies poor Nick Purden, from misery freed,
Who was a bookseller's hack:
He led such a damnable life in this world,–
I don't think he'll want to come back.'

The Art of Bookbinding
JOSEPH W. ZAEHNSDORF
1880

Buy good books, and read them; the best books are the commonest, and the last editions are always the best, if the editors are not blockheads.

PHILIP DORMER STANHOPE , 4TH EARL CHESTERFIELD
(1694–1773)

Selling books is nearly as bad as losing friends, than which life has no worse sorrow.

The Library
ANDREW LANG
(1844–1912)

Received a letter from Blackwood containing warm praise for *Adam Bede*, but wanting to know the rest of the story in outline before deciding whether it should go in the Magazine. I wrote in reply refusing to tell him the story.

Diary, 1st April 1858
GEORGE ELIOT
(1819–80)

Oh God of Gods in Zion! what a rushing river of joy gladdens my heart as often as I have a chance of going to Paris! There the days seem always short; there are the goodly collections on the delicate fragrant book-shelves.

The Love of Books
RICHARD DE BURY
(1281–1345)

Emma's religion, he [the curé] thought, might, from its fervour, end by touching on heresy, extravagance. But not being much versed in these matters, as soon as they went beyond a certain limit he wrote to Monsieur Boulard, bookseller

to Monsignor, to send him 'something good for a lady who was very clever.' The bookseller, with as much indifference as if he had been sending off hardware to savages, packed up, pellmell, everything that was then the fashion in the pious book trade. There were little manuals in questions and answers, pamphlets of aggressive tone after the manner of Monsieur de Maistre, and certain novels in rose-coloured bindings and with a honied style, manufactured by troubadour seminarists or penitent blue-stockings. There were the 'Think of it; the Man of the World at Mary's Feet, by Monsieur de ***, decorated with many Orders'; 'The Errors of Voltaire, for the Use of the Young,' etc. She read Balzac and George Sand, seeking in them imaginary satisfaction for her own desires. Even at table she had her book by her, and turned over the pages while Charles ate and talked to her.

Madame Bovary
GUSTAVE FLAUBERT
(1821–80)

Only works of great rarity or value should be full bound in morocco. If we have the luck to light on a Shakespeare quarto, on some master-piece of Aldus Manutius, by all means let us entrust it to the most competent binder, and instruct him to do justice to the volume. Let old English books, as More's *Utopia*, have a cover of stamped and blazoned calf. Let the binder clothe an early Rabelais or Marot ... in leather tooled with geometrical patterns. Let a Moliere or Corneille be bound in the graceful contemporary style... the lace-like pattern of the gilding resembles the Venetian point-lace, for which La Fontaine liked to ruin himself ... let panelled Russia leather array a folio of Shakespeare, and let English works of a hundred years ago be clothed in the sturdy fashion of Roger Payne.

The Library
ANDREW LANG
(1844–1912)

88

I lately met with an old volume from a London bookshop, containing the Greek Minor Poets, and it was a pleasure to read once more only the words Orpheus, Linus, Musæus, – those faint poetic sounds and echoes of a name, dying away on the ears of us modern men; and those hardly more substantial sounds, Mimnermus, Ibycus, Alcæus, Stesichorus, Menander. They lived not in vain. We can converse with these bodiless fames without reserve or personality.

A Week on the Concord and Merrimack Rivers
HENRY DAVID THOREAU
(1817–62)

In 1771, this notorious beauty [Madame Du Barry] could scarcely read or write … At Versailles, Madame Du Barry heard of the literary genius of Madame de Pompadour. The Pompadour was a person of taste. Her large library of some four thousand works of the lightest sort of light literature was bound by Biziaux … and to hear of these things excited the emulation of Madame Du Barry. She might not be CLEVER, but she could have a library like another, if libraries were in

fashion. One day Madame Du Barry astonished the Court by announcing that her collection of books would presently arrive at Versailles. Meantime she took counsel with a bookseller, who bought up examples of all the cheap 'remainders,' as they are called in the trade, that he could lay his hands upon. The whole assortment, about one thousand volumes in all, was hastily bound in rose morocco, elegantly gilt, and stamped with the arms of the noble house of Du Barry.

The Library
ANDREW LANG
(1844–1912)

How long would most people look at the best book before they would give the price of a large turbot for it.

Sesame and Lilies
JOHN RUSKIN
(1819–1900)

Ten Golden Rules
for the Preservation of Books.

1 Avoid a dry heat as much as you would a damp atmosphere. The one destroys as much as the other. The forme will affect the binding and the latter the paper. When reading, keep all books from the influence of the fire. *Never* keep any books near the ceiling where the room is illuminated by gas.

2 Never wet your fingers in turning over the leaves, but turn them over from the head. Catch each succeeding leaf up by the fore finger on the top corner as near the foredge as possible.

3 Never put cards or folded documents into a book or it will break the back. Keep such things in a portfolio.

4   Never read during meals. Crumbs and grease are ruinous to books.

5   Never turn a corner down to keep a place, but put a piece of paper projecting at the head as a mark.

6   Never push or pull a book along the table. To avoid scratches put a book down flat and firmly, and take it up the same way.

7   Never pull books out of the shelves by the headband, or suffer them to stand long upon the foredge. In doing the former the back is apt to be pulled or forced, by the latter the back gets out of shape.

8 Always open a book in a gentle manner and with a reverent spirit, especially such as are newly bound and never confine the leaves with the points of the thumbs; in doing so it breaks the back. Lay it upon a flat surface, and open it lightly, pressing upon the open leaves, and taking a few sheets at a time; go through the book until the requisite freedom is obtained.

9 Always use a paper knife or folder to cut up the leaves of uncut books, so that the edges may be smooth and even.

10 Treat books gently, for they are friends that never change. We benefit by their advice, and they exact no confessions.

The Art of Bookbinding
JOSEPH W. ZAEHNSDORF
1880

The conditions of a well bound book may be tersely enumerated. The binding should unite solidity and elegance. The book should open easily, and remain open at any page you please. It should never be necessary, in reading, to squeeze back the covers; and no book, however expensively bound, has been properly treated, if it does not open with ease.

The Library
ANDREW LANG
(1844–1912)

A library has three kinds of enemies to be guarded against, viz.: insects, dampness, and rats or mice. Everyone knows how to guard against dampness and rats or mice. Several means are known how to keep insects at a distance. The first consists in the proper choice of woods: these are cedar; cypress, mahogany, sandal, or very dry and sound oak. All these are compact or of very strong aroma and are such as insects do not like to pierce.

The Art of Bookbinding
JOSEPH W. ZAEHNSDORF
1880

A crazy bookcase, placed before
A low-price dealer's open door;
Therein arrayed in broken rows
A ragged crew of rhyme and prose,
The homeless vagrants, waifs, and strays
Whose low estate this line betrays
(Set forth the lesser birds to lime)
YOUR CHOICE AMONG THESE BOOKS – ONE DIME!

Epilogue to the
Breakfast Table Series
OLIVER WENDELL HOLMES
(1809–94)

There was [when I was living in Paris] a very ancient man, who had a room above my apartment. His was a sad story; he had been tutor to a noble family but he had been abandoned by his employers in the upheavals of the Revolution. Fearing that their castle would be looted he had fled, taking with him some of the rarest volumes in their library. Now, in distressed circumstances he was selling off his little hoard book by book, 'But do not pity me' he said, 'all I sell is the binding; the truth and poetry remain with me'; and he would tap his dry, old pate.

My Life in Paris and Rome
JAMES ARBUTHNOT
(1799–1880)

The sale of the library of a late learned prelate who had Boileau's hatred of a dull book was a scene to be avoided by his literary friends. The Bishop always gave the works which were offered to him a fair chance. He read till he could read no longer, cutting the pages as he went, and thus his progress could be traced like that of a backwoodsman who 'blazes' his way through a primeval forest. The paper-knife generally ceased to do duty before the thirtieth page.

The Library
ANDREW LANG
(1844–1912)

Books are the money of literature, but only the counters of Science.

THOMAS HENRY HUXLEY
(1825–95)

Good books are frequently re-printed and therefore never rare; thus the price of a book is usually in inverse proportion to the value of its content.

DR ANTHONY BARDER
(1868–1925)

The Novel

*T*HE NOVEL *AS WE KNOW IT Is a fairly recent form; a trea-*
sury we can visit with infinite ease whenever we
wish. A small row of novels contains a galaxy of love
and passion and imagination.

How well I remember the delight, and wonder, and pleasure with which I read *Jane Eyre*, sent to me by an author whose name and sex were then alike unknown to me; the strange fascinations of the book; and how with my own work pressing upon me, I could not, having taken the volumes up, lay them down until they were read through!

Roundabout Papers
WILLIAM MAKEPEACE THACKERAY
(1811–63)

To W.M. Thackeray, Esq this work is respectfully inscribed by the author.

dedication
Jane Eyre
CHARLOTTE BRONTË
(1816–55)

Books are not life. They are only tremulations on the ether. But the novel as a tremulation can make the whole man alive tremble.

D.H. LAWRENCE
(1885–1930)

Fred's studies are not very deep ... he is only reading a novel.

Middlemarch
GEORGE ELIOT
(1819–80)

I never read a novel, they have so little real life and thought in them.

HENRY DAVID THOREAU
(1817–62)

What is a novel if not a conviction of our fellow-men's existence strong enough to take upon itself a form of imagined life clearer than reality and whose accumulated verisimilitude

102

of selected episodes puts to shame the pride of documentary history?

A Personal Record
JOSEPH CONRAD
(1857–1924)

If only the Creator, whoever he may be, had read a few novels before he made the earth, how much better and brighter life could have been

ANTOINE DE MOULINS
2004

As a general rule I find that the welcome I give to a new novel is in inverse proportion to its length.

AN ANONYMOUS CRITIC

'Oh! it is only a novel! ... only Cecelia or Camilla, or Belinda:' only some work in which the most thorough of human nature, the happiest deliniation of its varieties, the liveliest effusions of wit and humour are conveyed to the world in the best chosen language.

Northanger Abbey
JANE AUSTEN
(1775–1817)

The novel is the one bright book of life.

Phoenix
D.H. LAWRENCE
(1885–1930)

What a strange custom that is in modern lady novelists to make the men bully the women! In the time of Miss Porter and Madame D'Arblay, we have respect, profound bows and curtsies, graceful courtesy, from men to women. In the time of Miss Bronte, absolute rudeness.

Roundabout Papers
WILLIAM MAKEPEACE THACKERAY
(1811–63)

Anybody can write a three-volume novel. It merely requires a complete ignorance of both life and literature.

OSCAR WILDE
(1854–1900)

We cannot have heroes to dine with us. There are none. And were those heroes to be had, we should not like them ... the persons whom you cannot care for in a novel, because they are so bad, are the very same that you so dearly love in your life, because they are so good.

The Eustace Diamonds
ANTHONY TROLLOPE
(1815–82)

The only reason for the existence of a novel is that it does attempt to represent life.

HENRY JAMES
(1843–1916)

And here lies the vast importance of the novel, properly handled. It can inform and lead into new places the flow of our sympathetic consciousness and it can lead our sympathy away in recoil from things gone dead.

Lady Chatterly's Lover
D.H. LAWRENCE
(1885–1930)

How do you like your novels? I like mine strong, 'hot with,' and no mistake: no love-making: no observations about society: little dialogue, except where the characters are bullying each other: plenty of fighting: and a villain in the cupboard, who is to suffer tortures just before Finis. I don't like your melancholy Finis. I never read the history of a consumptive heroine twice.

Roundabout Papers
WILLIAM MAKEPEACE THACKERAY
(1811–63)

It is the test of a novel writer's art that he conceal his snake-in-the-grass; but the reader may be sure that it is always there.

ANTHONY TROLLOPE
(1815–82)

Is it a book you would even wish your wife or your servants to read?

(of *Lady Chatterley's Lover,* while appearing
for the prosecution at the Old Bailey)
The Times, 21st October 1960
MERVYN GRIFFITH-JONES, British lawyer
(1909–79)

Avoid all kinds of pleasantry and facetiousness in thy discourse with her, and ... suffer her not to look into Rabelais, or Scarron, or *Don Quixote* – They are all books which excite laughter; and ... there is no passion so serious, as lust.

advice on courtship
The Life and Opinions of Tristram Shandy, Gentleman
LAURENCE STERNE
(1713–68)

He is a wonderfully accomplished man – most extraordinarily accomplished – reads – hem – reads every novel that comes out; I mean every novel that – hem – that has any fashion in it, of course. The fact is, that he did find so much in the books he read, applicable to his own misfortunes, and did find himself in every respect so much like the heroes – because of course he is conscious of his own superiority, as we all are, and very naturally – that he took to scorning everything, and became a genius.

Nicholas Nickleby
CHARLES DICKENS
(1812–70)

I will not adopt that ungenerous and impolitic custom so common with novel writers, of degrading by their contemptuous censure the very performances, to the number of which they are themselves adding – joining with their greatest enemies in bestowing the harshest epithets on such works, and scarcely ever permitting them to be read by their own heroine, who, if she accidentally take up a novel, is sure to turn over its insipid leaves with disgust.

Northanger Abbey
JANE AUSTEN
(1775–1817)

It is admitted that a novel can hardly be made interesting or successful without love ... It is necessary because the passion is one which interests or has interested all. Everyone feels it, has felt it, or expects to feel it.

Autobiography
ANTHONY TROLLOPE
(1815–82)

And then again about *Cranford*. I am so much pleased you like it. It is the only one of my own books that I can read again; but whenever I am ailing or ill, I take *Cranford* and – I was going to say *enjoy* it but that would not be pretty, – laugh over it afresh.

Letter to John Ruskin, 24 February 1865
ELIZABETH GASKELL
(1810–65)

It is an unfair advantage which the novelist takes of hero and heroine, as of his inexperienced reader, to say good-by to the two former, as soon as ever they are made husband and wife … A hero is much too valuable a gentleman to be put upon the retired list, in the prime and vigor of his youth; and I wish to know what lady among us would like to be put on the shelf, and thought no longer interesting, because she has a family growing up, and is four or five and thirty years of age? I have known ladies at sixty, with hearts as tender and ideas as romantic as any young misses of sixteen.

Roundabout Papers
WILLIAM MAKEPEACE THACKERAY
(1811–63)

I have this very moment finished reading a novel called *The Vicar of Wakefield* [by Oliver Goldsmith] ... It appears to me, to be impossible any person could read this book through with a dry eye and yet, I don't much like it ... There is but very little story, the plot is thin, the incidents very rare, the sentiments uncommon, the vicar is contented, humble, pious, virtuous – but upon the whole the book has not at all satisfied my expectations.

FRANCES BURNEY
(1752–1840)

The novel is a perfect medium for revealing to us the changing rainbow of our living relationships. The novel can help us to live, as nothing else can: no didactic Scripture, anyhow. If the novelist keeps his thumb out of the pan.

D.H. LAWRENCE
(1885–1930)

When I exclaim against novels, I mean when contrasted with those works which exercise the understanding and regulate the imagination. – For any kind of reading I think better than leaving a blank still a blank, because the mind must receive a degree of enlargement and obtain a little strength by a slight exertion of its thinking powers.

A Vindication of the Rights of Woman
MARY WOLLSTONECRAFT
(1759–97)

The novel is the highest form of human expression so far attained.

D.H. LAWRENCE
(1885–1930)

But Dr Johnson's approbation! – it almost crazed me with agreeable surprise – it gave me such a flight of spirits, that I danced a jig to Mr Crisp, without any preparation, music or explanation…

Mrs Thrale told him [Fanny Burney's father] that when he gave her the first volume of *Evelina*, which she had lent him, he said, 'Why, what a charming book you lent me!' and eagerly enquired after the rest.

Diary, 3rd August 1778
FANNY BURNEY
(1752–1840)

Every novel is a debtor to Homer.

RALPH WALDO EMERSON
(1803–82)

A novel has got to be pretty good these days to be better than the film.

PENELOPE WILDER
2000

But then in novels the most indifferent hero comes out right at last. Some god comes out of a theatrical cloud and leaves the poor devil ten thousand-a-year and a title.

Ayala's Angel
ANTHONY TROLLOPE
(1815–82)

In the middle of every night I wake up with an idea for a blockbuster, at breakfast it's a short story and by bedtime it's barely a joke.

ANONYMOUS ASPIRING AUTHOR

'It always is right in the novels. That's why I don't like them. They are too sweet. That's why I do like them, because they are so sweet. A sermon is not to tell you what you are, but what you ought to be, and a novel should tell you not what you are to get, but what you'd like to get.'

The Small House at Allington
ANTHONY TROLLOPE
(1815–82)

I wish you would not let him plunge into a vortex of Dissipation. I do not object to the Thing, but I cannot bear the expression; it is such thorough novel slang – and so old, that I dare say Adam met with it in the first novel he opened.

Letter to her neice
JANE AUSTEN
(1775–1817)

I spoke to him [Macaulay] once about *Clarissa*. 'Not read *Clarissa*' he cried out. 'If you have once thoroughly entered on *Clarissa* and are infected by it, you can't leave it. When I was in

India I passed one hot season at the hills, and there were the Governor-General, and the Secretary of Government, and the Commander-in-Chief, and their wives. I had *Clarissa* with me: and, as soon as they began to read, the whole station was in a passion of excitement about Miss Harlowe and her misfortunes, and her scoundrelly Lovelace! The Governor's wife seized the book, and the Secretary waited for it, and the Chief Justice could not read it for tears!' He acted the whole scene: he paced up and down the 'Athenaeum' library: I dare say he could have spoken pages of the book!

Roundabout Papers
WILLIAM MAKEPEACE THACKERAY
(1811–63)

The novels are as useful as Bibles, if they teach you the secret, that the best of life is conversation, and the greatest success is confidence, or perfect understanding between sincere people.

The Conduct of Life
RALPH WALDO EMERSON
(1803–82)

O leave novels, ye Mauchline belles,
    Ye're safer at your spinning-wheel;
Such witching books are baited hooks
    For rakish rooks, like Rob Mossgiel;
Your fine Tom Jones and Grandisons,
    They make your youthful fancies reel;
They heat your brains, and fire your veins,
    And then you're prey for Rob Mossgiel.

Beware a tongue that's smoothly hung,
    A heart that warmly seems to feel;
That feeling heart but acts a part –
    'Tis rakish art in Rob Mossgiel.
The frank address, the soft caress,
    Are worse than poisoned darts of steel;
The frank address, and politesse,
Are all finesse in Rob Mossgiel.

'O Leave Novels!'
Poems and Songs
ROBERT BURNS
(1759–56)

Read the conclusion, for the fiftieth time (I have read all W. Scott's novels at least fifty times), of the third series of Tales of my Lanlord – grand work – Scotch.

Fielding, as well as great English poet –
wonderful man! I long to get drunk with him

Diary, 5th January 1821
LORD BYRON
(1788–1824)

One should not be too severe on English
novels; they are the only relaxation of the
intellectually unemployed.

OSCAR WILDE
(1854–1900)

Bless my soul, Sir, will you Britons not credit that an American can be a gentleman, & have read the Waverly Novels, tho every digit may have been in the tar-bucket?

To his publisher, John Murray
HERMAN MELVILLE
(1819–91)

There was a literary gentleman present who who had dramatised in his time two hundred and forty-seven novels as fast as they had come out – and who was a literary gentleman in consequence.

Nicholas Nickleby
CHARLES DICKENS
(1812–70)

When I want to read a novel, I write one.

BENJAMIN DISRAELI
LORD BEACONSFIELD
(1804–81)

I got as far as the death of Mrs Lessway in *Hilda Lessways* on Sunday afternoon, and sent off the stuff as a specimen to Pinker yesterday. 33,000 words.

Diary, 15th February 1911
ARNOLD BENNETT
(1867–1931)

Finished *Jane Eyre*, which is really a wonderful book very peculiar in parts, but so powerfully and admirably written, such a fine tone in it, such fine religious feeling, and such beautiful writing. The descriptions of the mysterious maniac's nightly appearances awfully thrilling.

Diary, 23rd November 1880
QUEEN VICTORIA
(1819–1901)

For a novel addressed by a man to men and women of full age; which attempts to deal un-affectedly with the fret and fever, derision and disaster, that may press in the wake of the strongest passion known to humanity; to tell, without a mincing of words, of a deadly war waged between flesh and spirit; and to point the tragedy of unfulfill-ed aims, I am not aware that there is anything in the handling to which exception can be taken.

THOMAS HARDY
(1840–1928)

Here, my dear Lucy, hide these books. Quick, quick! Fling *Peregrine Pickle* under the toilette – throw *Roderick Random* into the closet – put *The Innocent Adultery* into *The Whole Duty of Man*; thrust *Lord Aimworth* under the sofa! cram *Ovid* behind the bolster; there – put *The Man of Feeling* into your pocket. Now for them.

The Rivals
RICHARD BRINSLEY SHERIDAN
(1751–1816)

The Novel

As I opened the front door this morning to leave from the office, the postman put a parcel in my hand. It was from John Lane, and it contained the first copy of my first book. I untied it hastily, and after glancing at the cover, gave it to Tertia to read. Tonight I looked through the tale, picking out my favourite bits.

Diary, 16th February 1898
ARNOLD BENNETT
(1867–1931)

If a novel reveals true and vivid relationships, it is a moral work, no matter what the relationships consist in. If the novelist honours the relationship in itself, it will be a great novel.

D.H. LAWRENCE
(1885–1930)

The Library

WHAT A PLEASURE IT must have been in the past to sit in one's library, by the window overlooking the deer in the park, and dip into the latest volume of Sterne or Fielding, just arrived from London. But equal intellectual delight can be afforded by a shelf full of well chosen paperbacks.

All men like to be their own librarians.

CHARLES DIBDIN
(1745–1814)

I go into my library, and all history unrolls before me. I breathe the morning air of the world while the scent of Eden's roses yet lingered ...

ALEXANDER SMITH
(1830–67)

The Ptolemies ... were thieves on a large scale. A department of the Alexandrian Library was called 'The Books from the Ships,' and was filled with rare volumes stolen from passengers in vessels that touched at the port. True, the owners were given copies of their ancient MSS., but the exchange ... was an 'involuntary' one, and not distinct from robbery.

The Library
ANDREW LANG
(1844–1912)

I undertake not to kindle a flame within this library.

Oath sworn by those wishing to read in the
Bodleian Library in Oxford

A man's library is a sort of harem.

RALPH WALDO EMERSON
(1803–82)

Every library should try to be complete on something, if it were only the history of pinheads.

OLIVER WENDELL HOLMES
(1809–94)

Many Londoners – not all – have seen the British Museum Library. I speak *a coeur ouvert*, and pray the kindly reader to bear with me. I have seen all sorts of domes of Peters and Pauls, Sophia, Pantheon, – what not? – and have been struck by none of them so much as by that catholic dome in Bloomsbury, under which our million volumes are housed. What peace, what love, what truth, what beauty, what happiness for all, what generous kindness for you and me, are here spread out!

Roundabout Papers
WILLIAM MAKEPEACE THACKERAY
(1811–63)

An assortment of broadsheet ballads and scrap-books, bought in boyhood, was the nucleus of Scott's library, rich in the works of poets and magicians, of alchemists, and anecdotists.

The Library
ANDREW LANG
(1844–1912)

The great British Library – an immense collection of volumes of all ages and languages, many of which are now forgotten, and most of which are seldom read.

The Art of Book-Making
WASHINGTON IRVING
(1783–1859)

What do we, as a nation, care about books? How much do you think we spend altogether on our libraries, public or private, as compared with what we spend on our horses?

JOHN RUSKIN
(1819–1900)

Give me the room whose every nook
Is dedicated to a book:
Two windows will suffice for air
And grant the light admission there, –
The eastern wall from frieze to plinth
Shall be the Poet's labyrinth,
Where one may find the lords of rhyme
From Homer's down to Dobson's time;
And at the northern side a space
Shall show an open chimney-place,
Set round with ancient tiles that tell
Some legend old, and weave a spell
The volumes on this wall should be
All prose and all philosophy,
From Plato down to those who are
The dim reflections of that star;
Upon the shelves along the west
The scientific books shall rest;
Beside them, History; above,
Religion, – hope, and faith, and love:
Lastly, the southern wall should hold
The story-tellers, new and old;
Haroun al Raschid, who was truth
And happiness to all my youth.

'The Library'
FRANK DEMPSTER SHERMAN
(1860–1916)

I am presented with the key of the book-case – So I go twisting and turning the said key into its rusty lock, and ouf! the fust and the must when the book-case is opened! Then what a search for something one can read through in less than a twelvemonth. Out of every hundred volumes, there are scarcely more than six or seven works ... The reason is, that country-house libraries are generally heir-looms, originally collected as a mark of gentility ... They consist of what are called standard books – books that would let the world stand still to the end of time! – composed and collected when knowledge ... was weighed out by the stone, or measured by the yard.

The Book of the Boudoir
LADY MORGAN
(1783–1859)

We have doubled the fines; banned smoking, drinking and eating and removed all but two hard chairs. I really don't know what more we can do to deter the punters.

A LIBRARIAN
c.1991

No furniture so charming
as books.

REV SYDNEY SMITH
(1771–1845)

In his library he had been always sure of leisure
and tranquillity; and though prepared ... to
meet with folly and conceit in every other room
in the house, he was used to be free of them there.

Pride and Prejudice
JANE AUSTEN
(1775–1817)

131

Meek young men grow up in libraries, believing it their duty to accept the views which Cicero, which Locke, which Bacon, have given, forgetful that Cicero, Locke, and Bacon were only young men in libraries, when they wrote these books. Hence, instead of Man Thinking, we have the book-worm.

RALPH WALDO EMERSON
(1803–82)

Madam, a circulating library in a town is as an evergreen tree of diabolical knowledge; it blossoms through the year.

RICHARD BRINSLEY SHERIDAN
(1751–1816)

The bookman cannot content himself with a selected library. He wants, as a minimum, a library reasonably complete in all departments. With such a basis acquired, he can afterwards wander into those special byways of book-buying which happen to suit his special predilections. Every Englishman who is interested in any branch of his native literature, and who respects himself, ought to own a comprehensive and inclusive library of English literature, in comely and adequate editions.

Literary Taste — How to Form It
ARNOLD BENNETT
(1867–1931)

Unlearned men of books assume the care,
As eunuchs are the guardians of the fair.

EDWARD YOUNG
(1683–1765)

Behind Mr. Osborne's dining-room was the usual apartment which went in his house by the name of the study; and was sacred to the master of the house. Hither Mr. Osborne would retire of a Sunday forenoon when not minded to go to church; and here pass the morning in his crimson leather chair, reading the paper. A couple of glazed book-cases were here, containing standard works in stout gilt bindings. *The Annual Register*, the *Gentleman's Magazine*, *Blair's Sermons*, and Hume and Smollett. From year's end to year's end he never took one of these volumes from the shelf; but there was no member of the family that would dare for his life to touch one of the books, except upon those rare Sunday evenings when there was no dinner-party, and when the great scarlet Bible and Prayer-book were taken out from the corner where they stood beside his copy of the *Peerage*, and the servants being rung up to the dining parlour, Osborne read the evening service to his family in a loud grating pompous voice. No member of the household, child, or domestic, ever entered that room without a certain terror.

Vanity Fair
WILLIAM MAKEPEACE THACKERAY
(1811–63)

In a library we are surrounded by many hundreds of dear friends, but they are imprisoned by an enchanter in these paper and leathern boxes.

RALPH WALDO EMERSON
(1803–82)

Come and take choice of all my library,
And so beguile thy sorrow.

Titus Andronicus
WILLIAM SHAKESPEARE
(1564–1616)

The true university of these days is a collection of books.

THOMAS CARLYLE
(1795–1881)

Twenty-two acknowledged concubines, and a library of sixty-two thousand volumes, attested the variety of his inclinations, and from the productions which he left behind him, it appears that the former as well as the latter were designed for use rather than ostentation.

The Decline and Fall of the Roman Empire
EDWARD GIBBON
(1737–94)

Whatever the librarians may say, there can be no true silence in a library while there are readers to whom the books gently murmur their cherished secrets.

CEDRIC SMYTHE
(1890–1917)

Such be the library; and take
This motto of a Latin make
To grace the door through which I pass:
Hic habitat Felicitas! [Here happiness resides]

'The Library'
FRANK DEMPSTER SHERMAN
(1860–1916)

In any library the most tatty and dog-eared books are most popular; those with unmarked jackets and virgin white pages are to be avoided.

TERRY MULL
(1918–57)

At any time I always have at least three books which I am reading. I like to have Penguin, or similar sized book, that will fit in my pocket, to read on buses and the tube; I like to have an intelligent book – a serious novel or biography – that I can read in an armchair in the evening and I like a diary or collection of short pieces to read in bed so that if I fall asleep I will not lose the thread of the author's thought.

GILBERT FARRER
(1920–87)

The best libraries are those in old schools where no one has had the time or wish to weed through the shelves and discard the old and unfashionable. Here you will find any number of delights and treasures.

James Hill
1965

I count it a great blessing that while I can remember the names of books and authors I enjoy and admire, I can forget the contents almost as soon as I have read them and thus can look forward to the pleasure of taking them down from the shelf and re-reading them almost immediately.

Anthony Weston
1985

'Man wants but little here below.'
LITTLE I ask; my wants are few;
   I only wish a hut of stone
(A very plain brown stone will do)
   That I may call my own; –
And close at hand is such a one,
In yonder street that fronts the sun.

Of books but few, – some fifty score
   For daily use, and bound for wear;
The rest upon an upper floor; –
   Some little luxury there
Of red morocco's gilded gleam
And vellum rich as country cream.

'Contentment'
OLIVER WENDELL HOLMES
(1809–94)

'Do you know what your wife wants?' replied Madame Bovary senior. 'She wants to be forced to occupy herself with some manual work. If she were obliged, like so many others, to earn her living, she wouldn't have these vapours, that come to her from a lot of ideas she stuffs into her head, and from the idleness in which she lives.'

'Yet she is always busy,' said Charles.

'Ah! always busy at what? Reading novels, bad books, works against religion, and in which they mock at priests in speeches taken from Voltaire. But all that leads you far astray, my poor child. Anyone who has no religion always ends by turning out badly.'

So it was decided to stop Emma reading novels. The enterprise did not seem easy. The good lady undertook it. She was, when she passed through Rouen, to go herself to the lending-library and represent that Emma had discontinued her subscription. Would they not have a right to apply to the police if the librarian persisted all the same in his poisonous trade?

Madame Bovary
GUSTAVE FLAUBERT
(1821–80)

Nothing sickens me more than the closed door of a library.

BARBARA TUCHMAN
On raising funds for New York
Public Library

Consider what you have in the smallest chosen library. A company of the wisest and wittiest men that could be picked out of all civil countries.

RALPH WALDO EMERSON
(1803–82)

... My library `
Was dukedom large enough.

The Tempest
WILLIAM SHAKESPEARE
(1564–1616)

No place affords a more striking conviction of the vanity of human hopes than a public library.

SAMUEL JOHNSON
(1709–84)

Books by the metre, books by the score
Nicely bound in leatherette and arranged from
ceiling to floor.
Haven't a clue what's in them
Reading is such a bore
But they're just the perfect shade of blue to go
with my new décor.

P.J.M.

With books and money plac'd for show
Like nest-eggs to make clients lay,
And for his false opinion pay.

SAMUEL BUTLER
(1612–80)

Unto my books so good to turn
Far ends of tired days;
It half endears the abstinence,
And pain is missed in praise.

As flavors cheer retarded guests
With banquetings to be,
So spices stimulate the time
Till my small library.

It may be wilderness without,
Far feet of failing men,
But holiday excludes the night,
And its bells within.

I thank these kinsmen of the shelf;
Their countenances bland
Enamour in prospective,
And satisfy, obtained.

EMILY DICKINSON
(1830–86)

If I invite my firends to dinner they would never think to ask if they could borrow my glasses or my silver; why then did they consider it socially permissible to ask if they can borrow books from my library; especially when they know and I know, they have only the smallest thought of ever returning them.

Letter
FREDERICK SELLARS, Bibliophile

Books constitute capital. A library book lasts as long as a house, for hundreds of years. It is not, then, an article of mere consumption but fairly of capital, and often in the case of professional men, setting out in life, it is their only capital.

THOMAS JEFFERSON
(1743–1826)

We call ourselves a rich nation, and we are filthy and foolish enough to thumb each other's books out of circulating libraries!

JOHN RUSKIN
(1819–1900)

Well, well, the wisest bend to Fate.
My brown old books around me wait,
My pipe still holds, unconfiscate,
    Its wonted station.
Pass me the wine. To Those that keep
The bachelor's secluded sleep
Peaceful, inviolate, and deep,
    I pour libation.

'A Gage D'Amour'
AUSTIN DOBSON
(1840–1921)

What a sad want I am in of libraries, of books to gather facts from! Why is there not a Majesty's library in every county town? There is a Majesty's jail and gallows in every one.

THOMAS CARLYLE
(1795–1881)

In an old library the better the binding, the more tedious the book.

ALFRED COGGINS
(1896–1940)

Books are like imprisoned souls till someone takes them down from a shelf and frees them.

SAMUEL BUTLER
(1835–1902)

Medicine for the soul.
Inscription over the door of the Library at Thebes
DIODORUS SICULUS

What is the world coming to when you can read *Lady Chatterly's Lover* for nothing in any public library but you have to pay for the glasses to do it with.

REV EDWARD JOB
(1928–87)

The Author and The Muse

*P*ITY THE POOR AUTHOR *pounding his keyboard and wondering if anyone will ever read his books and share his thoughts. So, give yourself a big pat on the back every time you buy a book.*

I have discovered that I cannot burn the candle at one end and write a book with the other.

Diary, 10th June 1919
KATHERINE MANSFIELD
(1888–1923)

Mrs. Timmins is a very pretty poetess (her 'Lines to a Faded Tulip' and her 'Plaint of Plinlimmon' appeared in one of last year's *Keepsakes*); and Fitzroy, as he impressed a kiss on the snowy forehead of his bride, pointed out to her, in one of the innumerable pockets of the desk, an elegant ruby-tipped pen, and six charming little gilt blank books, marked 'My Books,' which Mrs. Fitzroy might fill, he said (he is an Oxford man, and very polite), 'with the delightful productions of her Muse.'

A Little Dinner at Timmins's
WILLIAM MAKEPEACE THACKERAY
(1811–63)

My main wish is to get my books into other people's rooms, and to keep other people's books out of mine.

SAMUEL BUTLER
(1835–1902)

I feel a kind of reverence for the first books of young authors. There is so much aspiration in them, so much audacious hope and trembling fear, so much of the heart's history, that all errors and shortcomings are for a while lost sight of in the amiable self assertion of youth.

Drift-Wood
HENRY WADSWORTH LONGFELLOW
(1807–82)

An author who speaks about his own books is almost as bad as a mother who talks about her own children.

BENJAMIN DISRAELI
LORD BEACONSFIELD
(1804–81)

If people like to read their books, it is all very well, but to be at so much trouble in filling great volumes, which, as I used to think, nobody would willingly ever look into, to be labouring only for the torment of little boys and girls, always struck me as a hard fate.

Northanger Abbey
JANE AUSTEN
(1775–1817)

O let my books be then the eloquence
And dumb presagers of my speaking breast.

WILLIAM SHAKESPEARE
(1564–1616)

153

Writing or printing is like shooting with a rifle; you may hit your reader's mind, or miss it; but talking is like playing at a mark with the pipe of an engine; if it is within reach, and you have time enough, you can't help hitting it.

The Autocrat at the Breakfast Table
OLIVER WENDELL HOLMES
(1809–94)

One sheds one's sicknesses in books – repeats and presents again one's emotions, to be master of them.

D.H. LAWRENCE
(1885–1930)

So far as I am individually concerned, & independent of my pocket, it is my earnest desire to write those sort of books which are said to 'fail.'

HERMAN MELVILLE
(1819–91)

A talented lady from Rome
Decided to write a fat tome
But when only ten pages
Had taken her ages
Converted it into a pome.

P.J.M.

Authors have established it as a kind of rule, that a man ought to be dull sometimes; as the most severe reader makes allowances for many rests and nodding-places in a voluminous writer.

JOSEPH ADDISON
(1672–1719)

What these perplexities of my uncle Toby were, – 'tis impossible for you to guess; if you could, – I should blush ... as an author; inasmuch as I set no small store by myself upon this very account, that my reader has never yet been able to guess at any thing. And ... if I thought you was able to form the least ... conjecture to yourself, of what was to come in the next page, – I would tear it out of my book.

The Life and Opinions of Tristram Shandy
LAURENCE STERNE
(1713–68)

Anyone can think of a story; what the muse gives us are the words and insight with which to give it life and truth.

Notebooks and Diaries
ANTON MÜLLER
(1791–1872)

I have no ambition to surprise my reader. Castles with unknown passages are not compatible with my homely muse.

The Bertrams
ANTHONY TROLLOPE
(1815–82)

Quotation ... A writer expresses himself in words that have been used before because they give his meaning better than he can give it himself, or because they are beautiful or witty, or because he expects them to touch a cord of association in his reader, or because he wishes to show that he is learned and well read. Quotations due to the last motive are invariably ill-advised; the discerning reader detects it and is contemptuous; the undiscerning is perhaps impressed, but even then is at the same time repelled, pretentious quotations being the surest road to tedium.

A Dictionary of Modern English Usage
HENRY W. FOWLER
(1859–1933)

Thoroughly to unfold the labyrinths of the human mind is an arduous task … In order to dive into those recesses and lay them open to the reader in a striking and intelligible manner, 'tis necessary to assume a certain freedom in writing, not strictly perhaps within the limits prescribed by rules.

The Cry: A New Dramatic Fable
SARAH FIELDING
(1710–68)

I am extremely spiritless, dead and hopeless about my writing. The long state of headaches has left me in depression and incapacity.

GEORGE ELIOT
(1819–80)

For an author to write as he speaks is just as reprehensible as the opposite fault, to speak as he writes; for this gives a pedantic effect to what he says, and at the same time makes him hardly intelligible.

The Art of Literature
ARTHUR SCHOPENHAUER
(1788–1860)

The author himself is the best judge of his own performance; none has so deeply meditated on the subject; none is so sincerely interested in the event.

EDWARD GIBBON
(1737–94)

I should like to write a nightcap book – a book that you can muse over, that you can smile over, that you can yawn over – a book of which you can say, 'Well, this man is so and so and so and so; but he has a friendly heart'.

Roundabout Papers
WILLIAM MAKEPEACE THACKERAY
(1811–63)

No author, without a trial, can conceive of the difficulty of writing a romance about a country where there is no shadow, no antiquity, no mystery, no picturesque and gloomy wrong, nor anything but a commonplace prosperity, in broad and simple daylight, as is happily the case with my dear native land.

The Marble Faun
NATHANIEL HAWTHORNE
(1804–64)

L ast night I finished my sensational novel, *The Curse of Love*, 50,000 words in exactly three months, with all my other work. The writing of it has enormously increased my facility, and I believe that now I could do a similar novel in a month. It is, of the kind, good stuff, well written and well contrived, and some of the later chapters are really imagined and, in a way, lyrical. I found the business, after I had got into it, easy enough, and I rather enjoyed it. I could comfortably write 2,500 words in half a day. It has only been written once, and on revision, I have scarcely touched the original draft. Now I want to do two short stories – and then to my big novel.

Diary, 24th January 1899
ARNOLD BENNETT
(1867–1931)

G ood God! what a genius I had when I wrote that book.

Speaking of *A Tale of a Tub*
JONATHAN SWIFT
(1667–1745)

My books are water; those of the great geniuses is wine. Everybody drinks water.

MARK TWAIN
(1835–1910)

Writing, when properly managed … is but a different name for conversation: As no one … would venture to talk all; so no author, who understands the just boundaries of decorum and good breeding, would presume to think all: The truest respect which you can pay to the reader's understanding, is to … leave him something to imagine, in his turn, as well as yourself.

The Life and Opinions of Tristram Shandy, Gentleman
LAURENCE STERNE
(1713–68)

An author must be nothing if he do not love truth; a barrister must be nothing if he do.

The Bertrams
ANTHONY TROLLOPE
(1815–82)

Every other author may aspire to praise; the lexicographer can only hope to escape reproach, and even this negative recompense has been yet granted to very few.

Dictionary of the English Language
SAMUEL JOHNSON
(1709–84)

That author who draws a character, even though to common view incongruous in its parts, as the flying-squirrel, and, at different periods, as much at variance with itself as the caterpillar is with the butterfly into which it changes, may yet, in so doing, be not false but faithful to facts.

The Confidence-Man
HERMAN MELVILLE
(1819–91)

Of all human events, perhaps, the publication of a first volume of verses is the most insignificant; but though a matter of no moment to the world, it is still of some concern to the author.

Letter, May 22, 1860
HERMAN MELVILLE
(1819–91)

How pleasant to know Mr Lear!
Who has written such volumes of stuff!
Some think him ill-tempered and queer,
But a few think him pleasant enough.

Nonsense Songs
EDWARD LEAR
(1812–88)

Go, litel bok, go,
litel myn tragedye.

Troilus and Criseyde
GEOFFREY CHAUCER
(c.1343–1400)

Bodily offspring I do not leave, but mental offspring I do. Well, my books do not have to be sent to school and college, and then insist on going into the church, or take to drinking, or marry their mother's maid.

SAMUEL BUTLER
(1835–1902)

Chekhov made a mistake in thinking that if he had had more time he would have written more fully, described the rain, and the midwife and the doctor having tea. The truth is one can get only so *much* into a story; there is always a sacrifice. One has to leave out what one knows and longs to use. Why? I haven't any idea, but there it is. It's always a kind of race to get in as much as one can before it *disappears*.

But time is not really in it. Yet wait. I don't understand even now. I am pursued by time myself. The only occasion when I ever felt at

leisure was while writing *The Daughters of the Late Colonel*. And then at the end I was so terribly unhappy that I wrote as fast as possible for fear of dying before the story was sent. I should like to prove this, to work at real leisure. Only thus can it be done.

Diary, 17th January 1922
KATHERINE MANSFIELD
(1888–1923)

I feel my powers again, and this is, of itself, happiness; the eclipse of winter is passing from my mind. I shall again feel the enthusiastic glow of compositions, again, as I pour forth my soul upon paper, feel the winged ideas arise, and enjoy the delight of expressing them.

Diary, 18th June 1824
MARY SHELLEY
(1797–1851)

Book-Learning

*H*ERE IS A COCKTAIL OF *conflicting advice for any reader; should you follow Thoreau and read only what is best or should you follow Disraeli's advice and follow your heart wherever it leads?*

When my books are published it is as if I were dispatching a satellite to a distant galaxy: I have no idea whether my ideas will be understood, or even received, by anyone at all

JAQUES DEVILLE
c.1989

I should like to see working women take up their pride; I should like to see them educating themselves, for education is the grand motive power in the advancement of all classes. And there are few conditions of life, whether it be passed at the counter or over the needle, in the work-room or at the home, where an intelligent young woman has not some opportunity of gaining information; from a book snatched up at rare intervals, a print-shop window glanced at, as she passes along the street – if she have a genuine wish for mental improvement, the true thirst after what is good and beautiful, there is little fear but that she will gradually attain her end.

A Woman's Thoughts About Women
DINAH MARIA MULOCK CRAIK
(1826–87)

M istresses are like books; if you pore upon them too much, they doze you and make you unfit for company; but if used discreetly, you are the fitter for conversation by 'em.

The Country Wife
WILLIAM WYCHERLEY
(1640–1716)

R ead the best books first, or you may not have a chance to read them at all.

HENRY DAVID THOREAU
(1817–62)

L earning is acquired by reading books; but the much more necessary learning, the knowledge of the world, is only to be acquired by reading men, and studying all the various editions of them.

PHILIP DORMER STANHOPE
4TH EARL CHESTERFIELD
(1694–1773)

Bookworm, break this sloth urbane;
A greater spirit bids thee forth
Than the gray dreams which thee detain.

RALPH WALDO EMERSON
(1803–82)

It is a paradox that we can only learn from books whose truth we lack the knowledge to judge: could we judge their value then we would already be wiser than their author.

JOHANN WOLFGANG VON GOETHE
(1749–1832)

You may judge a man's knowledge by the marginalia in his books.

Learning hath gained most by those books by which the printers have lost.

THOMAS FULLER
(1608–61)

How often when I was a student I had to race through the great literature of the world, and how often I wished I had the time to read leisurely, slowly and reflectively – in a word – with enjoyment.

DEBORAH DE FOIX
(1933–98)

The love of learning, the sequestered nooks,
And all the sweet serenity of books.

HENRY WADSWORTH LONGFELLOW
(1807–82)

Learning is, in too many cases, but a foil to common sense; a substitute for true knowledge. Books are less often made use of as 'spectacles' to look at nature with, than as blinds to keep out its strong light and shifting scenery from weak eyes and indolent dispositions … The learned are mere literary drudges.

WILLIAM HAZLITT
(1778–1830)

Whence is thy learning? Hath thy toil
O'er books consum'd the midnight oil?

JOHN GAY
(1685–1732)

M uch reading is an oppression of the mind, and extinguishes the natural candle, which is the reason of so many senseless scholars in the world.

WILLIAM PENN
(1644–1718)

A man ought to read just as inclination leads him; for what he reads as a task will do him little good.

BENJAMIN DISRAELI
LORD BEACONSFIELD
(1804–81)

I n their writings the Indian sages give many pre-dictions of the times when the rain will fall. But squeeze these books as strongly as you like, you will not obtain from them a single drop of water. Similarly, you cannot extract from all the most moral writings in the world a single good action.

LEO TOLSTOY
(1828–1910)

Read Homer once, and you can read no more;
For all books else appear so mean, so poor,
Verse will seem prose; but still persist to read,
And Homer will be all the books you need.

Essay on Poetry
DUKE OF BUCKINGHAM AND NORMANBY
(1649–1720)

R ead no history: nothing but biography,
for that is life without theory.

BENJAMIN DISRAELI
LORD BEACONSFIELD
(1804–81)

He has left off reading altogether, to the great improvement of his originality.

CHARLES LAMB
(1775–1834)

I skim through books, I do not learn from them. What I remember of them is what I have made of them; it is something I no longer recognize as coming from anyone other than myself.

MICHEL DE MONTAIGNE
(1533–92)

If you steal from one author, it's plagiarism; if you steal from many, it's research.

WILSON MIZNER
(1876–1933)

Books are never further from a mandarin's hand than a song is from a minstrel's lips.

CHINESE PROVERB

Life being very short, and the quiet hours of it few, we ought to waste none of them in reading valueless books.

JOHN RUSKIN
(1819–1900)

I always was of opinion that the placing a youth to study with an attorney was rather a prejudice than a help … The only help a youth wants is to be directed what books to read, and in what order to read them.

THOMAS JEFFERSON
(1743–1826)

The *Young Man's Best Companion*, *The Farrier's Sure Guide*, *The Veterinary Surgeon*, *Paradise Lost*, *The Pilgrim's Progress*, *Robinson Crusoe*, *Ash's Dictionary*, and *Walkingame's Arithmetic*, constituted his library; and though a limited series, it was one from which he had acquired more sound information by diligent perusal than many a man of opportunities had done from a furlong of laden shelves.

THOMAS HARDY
(1840–1928)

B ooks must follow sciences, and not sciences
books.

FRANCIS BACON
(1561–1626)

R eading is not a duty, and has consequently no
business to be made disagreeable.

AUGUSTINE BIRRELL
(1850–1933)

A ny reading not of a vicious species must be a
good substitute for the amusements too apt
to fill up the leisure of the labouring classes.

JAMES MADISON
(1751–1836)

R eading maketh a full man; conference a
ready man; and writing an exact man.

FRANCIS BACON
(1561–1626)

The learning we derive from books is like fire. We bring it home from our neighbour, blow it into life at home, pass it on to others, and thus its ownership becomes common currency.

FRANÇOIS MARIE AROUET DE VOLTAIRE
(1694–1778)

The book-worm wraps himself up in his web of verbal generalities, and sees only the glimmering shadows of things reflected from the minds of others.

Table-Talk Essays on Men and Manners
WILLIAM HAZLITT
(1778–1830)

Books are the meat of philosophers; they discuss them as butchers might discuss pigs.

CHINESE PROVERB

A prejudice, just because it is published in a *book*, is not immediately transmuted into an irrefutable and undeniable fact.

HANS LESSING
(1899–1959)

A reading machine, always wound up and going,
He mastered whatever was not worth the
knowing.

JAMES RUSSELL LOWELL
(1819–91)

A lawyer without books would be like a workman without tools.

THOMAS JEFFERSON
(1743–1826)

He has a quotation for every occasion, but a thought for none.

CHARLES NAPIER
(1874–1965)

The King to Oxford sent a troop of horse,
For Tories own no argument but force:
With equal skill to Cambridge books he sent,
For Whigs admit no force but argument.

WILLIAM BROWNE
(1692–1774)

The reading or non-reading a book will never keep down a single petticoat.

LORD BYRON
(1788–1824)

Authors and Critics

I AM MY OWN SEVEREST critic, said the smug author. Not while I am alive, you're not, replied the acid critic. This chapter explores the often troublesome relationship between the author and critic, both professional and otherwise.

When the author has no idea of what to reply to a critic he likes to say, 'I bet you could not have written it any better'. This is the same as if a taxi driver involved in an accident were to say to his blind passenger. 'I bet you couldn't have driven this far without a crash'.

HANS LESSING
(1899–1959)

An Author, when he first appears in the World, is very apt to believe it has nothing to think of but his Performances.

The Spectator
RICHARD STEELE
(1672–1729)

So you're the little woman who wrote the book that made this great war!

On being introduced to
Harriet Beecher Stowe
ABRAHAM LINCOLN
(1809–65)

America is now given over to a damned mob of scribbling women.

NATHANIEL HAWTHORNE
(1804–64)

I never read a book before reviewing it; it prejudices a man so.

SYDNEY SMITH
(1771–1845)

I went down to see Tennyson, who is very peculiar-looking, tall, dark, with a fine head, long black, flowing hair, and a beard; oddly dressed, but there is no affectation about him. I told him how much I admired his glorious lines to my precious Albert, and how much comfort I found in his In Memoriam. He was full of unbounded appreciation of beloved Albert. When he spoke of my own loss, of that to the nation, his eyes quite filled with tears.

Diary, 14th April 1862
QUEEN VICTORIA
(1819–1901)

It is a noble grand book, whoever wrote it – but Miss Evans' [George Eliot's] life taken at the best construction, does so jar against the beautiful book that one cannot help hoping against hope.

On first hearing of the true identity of George Eliot
ELIZABETH GASKELL
(1810–65)

187

Critics generally come to be critics not by reason of their fitness for this, but of their unfitness for anything else. Books should be tried by a judge and jury as though they were a crime, and counsel should be heard on both sides.

SAMUEL BUTLER
(1835–1902)

Formerly we used to canonise our heroes. The modern method is to vulgarise them. Cheap editions of great books may be delightful, but cheap editions of great men are absolutely detestable.

OSCAR WILDE
(1854–1900)

Can an author with reason complain that he is cramped and shackled if he is not at liberty to publish blasphemy, bawdry, or sedition? all of which are equally prohibited in the freest governments, if they are wise and well-regulated ones.

PHILIP DORMER STANHOPE, 4TH EARL CHESTERFIELD
(1694–1773)

A transition from an author's books to his conversation, is too often like an entrance into a large city, after a distant prospect. Remotely, we see nothing but spires of temples, and turrets of palaces, and imagine it the residence of splendor, grandeur, and magnificence; but, when we have passed the gates, we find it perplexed with narrow passages, disgraced with despicable cottages, embarrassed with obstructions, and clouded with smoke.

SAMUEL JOHNSON
(1709–84)

Whatever an author puts between the two covers of his book is public property; whatever of himself he does not put there is his private property, as much as if he had never written a word.

Country Living and Country Thinking
GAIL HAMILTON
(1833–96)

Dryden has himself told us that he was of a grave cast and did not much excel in sallies of humour. One of his bons mots, however, has been preserved. He does not seem to have lived on very amicable terms with his wife, Lady Elizabeth, whom, if we may believe the lampoons of the time, he was compelled by one of her brothers to marry. Thinking herself neglected by the bard, and that he spent too much time in his study, she one day exclaimed, 'Lord, Mr. Dryden, how can you always be poring over those musty books? I wish I were a book, and then I should have more of your company.' 'Pray, my dear,' replied old John, 'if you do become a book let it be an almanack, for then I shall change you every year.'

Anecdotes
SIR JAMES PRIOR
1860

A modern author would have died in infancy in a ruder age.

HENRY DAVID THOREAU
(1817–62)

You have observed a skilful man reading Virgil. Well, that author is a thousand books to a thousand persons. Take the book into your two hands, and read your eyes out; you will never find what I find.

RALPH WALDO EMERSON
(1803–82)

Ellen, I was crazy to read your book; but I never found anybody I could borrow it from!

Reportedly said by a friend to
ELLEN GLASGOW
(1874–1945)

A poet, as he is the author to others of the highest wisdom, pleasure, virtue, and glory, so he ought personally to be the happiest, the best, the wisest, and the most illustrious of men.

A Defence of Poetry
PERCY BYSSHE SHELLEY
(1792–1822)

To all, to each! a fair good-night,
And pleasing dreams, and slumbers light.

SIR WALTER SCOTT
(1771–1832)